Things I Wish
I Could've Told
Him

M. SOSA

First Printing, June 2018

ISBN: 978-0-9951533-8-7

"I held on to you because
there was always a piece of *hope*
left within me that believed
you'd come back…

someday."

"I finally made peace
with all the broken pieces
of my past, and forgiving myself
was the first step to
getting over you."

"I don't know why I stayed when
I knew how unhappy I was.
I guess my mistake was
staying longer than I should have."

"You know when you're tired of trying,
tired of not saying a word when things bother you,
tired of the restless nights, tired of pretending things
are okay, tired of holding on when you know
you should be letting go."

"I fight with myself daily
because I'm stuck believing
what my *heart* is feeling instead
of facing the truth and
believing my *mind*."

"Maybe I'm scared of starting over because I'm worried they'll end up hurting me *like you did*."

"The truth is
I still love you
and I probably always will.
I lie to everybody around me
because I don't want them
to know I'm still stuck on you.
Stupid in love."

"And just like that, *strangers* is all we were."

"The harsh reality is that you're gone
and you're not coming back.
I have to let our past go
if I want to feel *liberated*."

"There's nothing wrong in missing him.
There's nothing wrong in hoping.
There's nothing wrong in believing.
Just don't waste years of your life
holding on to a fantasy."

"The day will come when you remember
all the bullshit you put me through.
You'll remember how I stuck by you when nobody
else would and it'll hurt to know that you once had
somebody that *loved you unconditionally*."

"You had me,
and that was
always enough."

"The biggest lesson
I learned from you
was *knowing when to leave*
when a relationship felt dead."

"Thanks to you, I'm stronger than ever.
I no longer cry out your name in my sleep.
I don't blame myself for everything
that went wrong between us
because I know *I gave it my all*."

"Your friends said I was no good for you
because they never knew what a good woman was

...and you believed them."

"Even after you left,
I waited patiently for you to come back
until I noticed *you moved on without me*.
She was brand new, fresh meat,
someone that didn't know all your flaws.
She was your everything, while I was
nothing more than your *crazy ex.* "

"I took you back, over and over,
because I thought you'd change
but no matter how hard we tried,
you always showed your true colors
by *breaking my heart.*"

"There's nothing worse than a selfish man
that believes he is owed the world.
He mistreats his woman by ignoring her
wants and needs, and only puts his first.
Ignores her cry for help because he's too busy
living his life and forgets that *she's part of it too*."

"Sometimes, I wonder
if you *miss me* too."

"There's no point *denying* that
you miss someone when you know
they're all you can think about."

"*Time heals all wounds*
but sometimes,
the wounds are too deep
and feel like it'll take an eternity to fix."

"Nobody will ever understand all the love
I felt for you. They'll see me smiling and laughing,
living my best life without realizing how broken
I'm feeling inside.

Don't always believe everything you see."

"Do you know what it's like to feel violated,
disappointed, abandoned and love all at once,
and still want the person back even if
they don't feel the same way anymore?

I did, the day you left."

"Sometimes, I ask myself why I even bothered loving you so much when all you did was *break me down*."

"Not everyone is meant
to stay *forever*."

"Never put yourself in a situation
where you're always the one *chasing*."

"I stopped checking for you
because it hurt me more to see
what you were doing,

living happily without me."

"I couldn't move on because I kept
searching for you in everybody I met.
As much as I tried to move on with my life,
you *haunted me*. I would remember all the places we
went, the kisses we shared, your scent and most of all,
the agony of not having you by my side anymore."

"Remember when you told me forever?

They were all lies."

"I want to see you suffer and beg, like I did.
And maybe that won't be enough because I know it
won't change the fact that you'll never fully
comprehend the *humiliation you put me through*."

"There are times when I look up at the sky
and *gaze* at the stars way up above,
and I can't help but wonder
if you're *staring* at them too."

"Maybe I don't forgive you and it's all a *charade*.
It's a way to lie to myself in order to convince me that
I'm over you... when I'm clearly not."

"The one thing you'll never see me
do is beg for you to love me.
If you're not able to see my worth
and everything I bring to the table,
then you were never the *right man* for me."

"Someday, you'll remember a silly moment
we shared and tons of memories
will come flashing back.

Just knowing that puts a smile on my face."

"It's painful to *wait* for someone
but it's even harder to *forget*."

"The only reason we *fear* letting our ex go
is because we fear not knowing what comes next,
or maybe it's the fear of being *alone*."

"You didn't notice
but I finally cut the cord.
I *freed myself* of everything
you used to mean to me."

"Sometimes, the best thing you can
do is not obsess, not overthink.
Just believe *what's meant to be, will be.*"

"I gave you my word that
I'd stick by you forever.
I can see that *you* never meant it."

"So, I see you're having a baby with her.
Part of me is happy for you
and the other part hates you
because that *should have been me*."

"Just because he's confused
about what he wants doesn't mean
you have to waste your time waiting."

"I kept blaming myself for your mistakes
while you were out there living the happy life.
Selfish, that's all that you are
and all that you'll ever be."

"Maybe part of my *fantasy* was believing
that what we once had would
somehow happen again."

"I can't blame you for everything
because I knew exactly what *type of man* you were.
But, I chose to stay because I thought maybe,
just maybe, you would love me someday."

"Do you expect me to smile after
everything you did to me? I'm devastated.
I'm empty. I'm not the same. I spend days and night
awake wondering where you are and who you're
with. I'm restless. I'm anxious. I'm every word in the
book all bundled up in one. And through it all, I have
to wonder *if you ever even truly loved me*?"

"Anybody that can leave you,
without thinking twice about the pain
they're going to cause you,
isn't meant for you.
Let them go."

"You were *toxic* and I knew it,
but I still wanted you to come back."

"Someday, someone will look at me
with the same eyes you once did,
but *they'll stay… they'll stay.*"

"Stop investing your time and energy
on someone who isn't willing
to *treat you better*."

"You can't control who you love
but you are responsible for how someone treats you.
If you know they're not giving you what you deserve,
tell them and make sure they modify their behaviour
towards you. But, don't stay stuck hoping they'll
change if you're not able to communicate how you
feel. *You matter. Never forget that.*"

"Loving your potential was my downfall.
I should have known better than to
fall in love with a *pretty face*."

"The days felt so long when you left.
I counted every minute, every hour
hoping I'd see your face once more
but you were too busy to notice.
You were already dating someone new,
ignoring all the misery I was going through.
Shows what kind of man you are."

"*Unhealthy relationships*
shouldn't be worshipped.
Something that toxic
should be despised."

"If I gave you a second chance,
would you do the same things
or would you learn from your mistakes
and make the effort?

Decisions… decisions."

"You kept breaking my heart
and I kept going back
because you were all that I knew.
That's when it finally hit me
that I was the one *sabotaging myself*."

"I forgave your indiscretions,
pushed aside all the heartache
and accepted your false promises
because I didn't want to give up
on everything I had worked *so hard to build.*"

"You're wasting years of your life
with someone who continually hurts you,
instead of being with someone who *builds you up*."

"The pain of admitting *failure* is harder
than admitting what we once shared was a *farce*."

"Our relationship had no foundation.
I could've tried harder.
You could've believed more in us.
Half promises never fulfilled
and now everything
we have left are *memories*."

"Putting my life *back together*
was hard, knowing
you'd no longer
be a part of it."

"Everywhere I look, *you're all that I see.*
I remember all the good times we shared
instead of remembeing all the sorrow
you left me with."

"Can you blame me for being jealous
of your future lovers?

They'll get to experience
what my heart once felt."

"That's the thing about unconditional love,
you give without expecting anything back,
and maybe I'm inconsiderate for
expecting more from you."

"There's nothing I need more
than *loyalty* and *love*."

"Everything you did made me smile,
and I keep wondering if I'll ever see
that same *smile* again."

"*Potential* is a killer.
Don't stick around waiting for them
to be someone they're not."

"The only thing I'm focusing on right now
is *growing, healing*, and making sure I never
feel *helpless*. I'm building a stronger version of
myself and nobody is going to stand in my way."

"Will my heart skip a beat?
Will I start sweating tremendously?
Will you stop and talk, or
will you pass me by as if I don't exist?
Will you think of me all day
and wonder what could have been?
Will you call me and ask for forgiveness?
So many questions flood my mind
when I think of *bumping into you*."

"If the universe is
forcing him out your life,
let him go."

"There was never anything wrong with me.
You treated me poorly which shows
there was *something wrong with you* all along.
Anybody that loves you dearly doesn't
go around destroying people that love them."

"You lying, cheating,
irresponsible douchebag.
I can't believe I stuck around
waiting for you to come back."

"I lost myself loving you,
and now I have to find myself
and get reacquainted with *who I used to be.*"

"I should've listened when they
told me not to run back to my ex.
That shit didn't work out for a reason
but I guess being *foolishly in love*
makes you do the dumbest things."

"I don't have trust issues.
I have *YOU* issues."

"If he wants to walk away,
hold the door wide open
and let him go.
There's nothing worse
than *begging* someone
to stay when they don't value
what they're letting go of."

"You never deserved a place in my heart.
It was hard to accept but I see it now...

I see it clearly."

"You knew I'd stay no matter
what you said or did to me.
Your *narcissistic* ways blocked me
from seeing who you really were."

"I should've let you go
the moment I realized
you were *draining my happiness*."

"I got lost in your words until
I remembered your actions.
They always spoke louder
than your *false promises*."

"*Being a good woman to yourself*
is more important than being
a good woman to any man."

"I fell in love with the hallucination
of who you once were.
And everyday,
I realize everything I thought
I loved about you *isn't there anymore.*"

"*Maybe I don't miss you.*
Maybe I only miss the time I spent with you."

"The best decision you'll ever do for your heart,
your soul and your sanity is to leave
when someone is toxic.
There's no point in *fighting*
for someone who's constantly
making your life a living hell."

"When I stopped focusing
my energy on you,
I was able to focus that same energy
on *healing myself.*"

"One thing I learned a long time ago
was to never ignore the *red flags* in the beginning,
or they'll be the same reason it all ends."

"You kept crawling back into my life
because you were tired of the person
you tried to replace me with.

Shame on me for believing you actually cared."

"I kept breaking my heart,
taking him back, knowing he was
never going to change."

"I hope you find someone
who *loves you* the way I did."

"Did you ever think twice
about how I would feel after you left?
I guess not because you've never
checked up on me since."

"Heartbreak after heartbreak,
you'll eventually learn that not everybody
deserves to be *surrounded by you*."

"You can deny it all you want
but I know a little piece of me
will *always be with you.*"

"Parts of me long for your touch,
just want to feel your lips, your body,
one more time."

"I'm ashamed to admit how much I miss you.
I know I shouldn't be thinking about someone
who's caused me emotional distress but
you're the only one that knew me better
than I knew myself.

Maybe that's why I'm stuck thinking
about you all the time."

"I thought parts of me felt imcomplete
without you laying next to me,
but it was worse sleeping next to someone
that made me *feel alone*, each night."

"I forgive you.
You've moved on with someone else,
and even though years have passed,
you still cross my mind every now and then.
It's no longer love but I'm stuck on
who you used to be, and
I wonder if you're going to end up
hurting her the same way."

"*I knew.*
I just played stupid
to see if you'd be honest."

"I thought we were *unbreakable*
but your actions showed me otherwise."

"You kept treating me the way
you felt about yourself."

"Don't believe them
when they keep disappointing you.
You're nobody's fool.

"At the end of it all,
everything happened
the way it was supposed to.
There's a lesson in everything
I've been through, that helped me grow
and helped me heal.

Everything that I thought was
breaking me was actually shaping me
into the *wonder woman* I am today."

Instagram
www.instagram.com/sweetzthoughts

Facebook
www.facebook.com/sweetzthoughts

Things I Wish I Could've Told Him
2018

Made in the USA
Middletown, DE
06 October 2018